This book is the property of Sandra Hartl[illegible]
Return to Joshua Dryden -

EAGLE

EAGLE

Terrence N. Ingram

Foreword by Christine Sheppard

Principle Photography:
The Wildlife Collection

MetroBooks

MetroBooks

An Imprint of Friedman/Fairfax Publishers

Library of Congress Cataloging-in-Publication Data

Ingram, Terrence N.
Eagle / by Terrence N. Ingram.
p. cm.
Includes index.
ISBN 1-56799-558-6
1. Eagles. I. Title.
QL696.F32I54 1998
598.9'42—dc21 97-50147

Foreword and Captions: Christine Sheppard
Editors: Rachel Holzman and Reka Simonsen
Art Director: Jeff Batzli
Designer: Garrett Schuh
Photography Editor: Deidra Gorgos
Production Manager: Jeanne Hutter

Color separations by Fine Arts Repro House Co., Ltd.
Printed in China by Leefung-Asco Printers Ltd.

10 9 8 7 6 5 4 3 2 1

For bulk purchases and special sales, please contact:
Friedman/Fairfax Publishers
Attention: Sales Department
15 West 26th Street
New York, NY 10010
212/685-6610 FAX 212/685-1307

Visit our website:
http://www.metrobooks.com

PHOTOGRAPHY CREDITS

Corbis-Bettmann: p. 39

©Michael Friedman Publishing Group: p. 46

Visuals Unlimited: ©Bill Banaszewski: p.136; **©Ken Lucas:** p. 119; **©Joe McDonald:** pp. 106, 107; **©Kjell B. Sandved:** p. 28

The Wildlife Collection: ©Bob Bennett: pp. 90, 91; **©Rick and Nora Bowers:** pp. 96-97; **©Michael Francis:** pp. 6 left, 20, 44, 54 right, 62-63, 66, 68, 69, 76, 82, 85, 88, 89, 93, 94,100, 101,104, 111, 113, 122, 131; **©D. Robert Franz:** pp. 35, 38, 48, 54 left, 66-67, 70, 78, 79, 86, 108, 109, 111, 114, 116-117, 123, 127,135; **©Dennis Frieborn:** pp. 11, 87, 92, 98-99, 110, 130; **©Martin Harvey:** pp. 14, 15, 21, 22, 23, 31;**©Henry H. Holdsworth:** pp. 2, 9, 12, 16, 17, 36, 37, 41, 42-43, 45, 47, 51, 52-53, 55, 56, 57, 58-59, 60, 61, 64, 65, 71, 72-73, 74, 77, 80-81, 81 right, 83, 95, 105, 118, 120-121, 126, 128-129, 133, 138-139;**©Dean Lee:** pp. 14, 33; **©Jo Overholt:** pp. 50, 103,115; **©Ralph Lee Hopkins:** pp. 13; **©HPH Photography:** pp. 6-7, 24 both, 25, 26, 32, 141; **©Gary Schultz:** pp. 40, 75, 124-125; **©Jack Swenson:** pp. 29; **©Tom Vezo:** pp. 96 left, 137

ACKNOWLEDGMENTS

This book would never have flown without the dedication and hard work of the following people: Rachel Holzman, Reka Simonsen, Garrett Schuh, Kevin Ullrich, Paul Taurins, Deidra Gorgos, Jeff Batzli, and especially Christine Sheppard.

CONTENTS

FOREWORD

The King of Birds. The Lord of the Sky. Throughout time the eagle has been a symbol of power, strength, and freedom. In reality, however, like humans and all other animals, eagles must work to survive. Only in our imaginations are any living creatures free from the need to find food, a mate, safety from predators, and shelter from cold, wind, and rain. This book will show you the real world of eagles. You will explore the details of an eagle's life as it grows from egg to adult, and you will discover the fascinating diversity of the more than sixty species of eagles that are found almost all over the world.

What is an eagle? There is no technical, scientific definition. Dictionaries and encyclopedias define "eagle" as a large bird of prey, although some eagles are small and one is actually vegetarian. The English word "eagle" can be traced back to the Latin *aquila,* which was used by the Romans for the bird we call the golden eagle. Latin speakers traveling the globe might have called strange, new hunting birds *aquila,* and so the name came to refer to different birds in different places. In French, the word *aigle,* also derived from *aquila,* is used for some but not all of the birds we call eagles. The same is true for the German *adler,* which has a different root word.

In the eighteenth century, people interested in natural history and other sciences began to develop systems of classification: ways to group and perhaps explain similarities in animals, plants, and minerals. If one bird in a group was called an eagle, the entire group might be given that name, even though they varied in size and behavior. This helps explain the fact that the vulturine fish eagle, while a relative of the bald eagle, is vegetarian, and is also known as the palm nut vulture. Ultimately, the word "eagle" allows this book to explore a group of fascinating birds and their adaptations, behavior, and relationship with man.

Eagles live by hunting, and their bodies are perfectly designed for chasing and killing. They have heavy bodies relative to their size, which makes it absolutely necessary for them to have powerful wing muscles and wings constructed for high lift. Eagle wings are also built to perform at the slow speeds needed to patrol carefully for prey. An eagle's feet are equipped with sharp, strong talons and a grasp of steel—they are its killing tools and most dangerous weapons. The bill, with its cruel hook and razor-sharp edges, is used to tear and cut flesh, if prey is too large to swallow whole.

The most vulnerable stage of an eagle's life is the time spent in the nest, as an egg and as an eaglet. Snakes, monkeys, forest cats, and even other eagles relish an eaglet as a meal. Once flying, young eagles still have much to learn: how to land, how to hunt, and where to shelter from wind and weather. Parents teach their young the necessary survival skills, but eventually every eagle must go out on its own.

Why do we need eagles? To me, it is enough that the sight of an eagle in flight gives me joy and a share of the freedom, power, and pride that the birds embody. For those that need more convincing, there are other reasons.

Like the canary in the coal mine, eagles provide early warning when our environment becomes contaminated. Poisons from the environment enter plants, then became concentrated in animals that use plants as food. Birds of prey then feed on the plant-eating animals, concentrating the poisons even more. Through a food chain this simple, eagles get a heavy share of what was once dilute. Diminishing eagle populations in the 1970s caused concerned people to look more closely at pesticides and the danger they pose to both eagles and humans.

More fundamentally, eagles are part of ecosystems, and the effects of their loss may be unexpectedly dramatic. Without the hunters, prey populations may explode and consume more plants or seeds than is normal for an ecosystem. Without seeds and seedlings to replace lost trees and shrubs, whole plant communities, even forests, may disappear.

We share the world with eagles, and we also share their future. What happens to them will eventually happen to us. Eagles cannot reverse the changes humans have made or influence the direction that humans will take, but we, as humans, can do both. It is up to each of us to make sure that eagles have a bright future on a healthy, living planet, both for the eagles' sake and for our own.

Christine Sheppard
Curator, Wildlife Conservation Society
January 1998

INTRODUCTION

THE WHITE HEAD AND TAIL GLISTEN IN THE BRIGHT SUN, THE STRONG CLAWS WITH RAZOR-SHARP TALONS ARE CLENCHED FOR battle, and the powerful wings soar on the wind as the large bird pulls itself higher and higher into the blue sky. Broad wings reach out as the bird feels a strong current pushing on its feathers. It glides in circles as the air raises the bird heavenward. Intense proud eyes stare over the golden hooked beak as the great bird surveys its domain far below.

This is the romantic image that most Americans have of the national symbol, the bald eagle. And it is, in fact, more than just a fantasy. It is a reality observed by thousands of people throughout the year as they witness one of nature's greatest thrills—seeing a bald eagle in the wild.

But the bald eagle is only one of many species commonly called "eagle." Although most people know what is meant by the word "eagle," it is not a biological term. It is, rather, a layperson's name that is used for a variety of birds that are not necessarily closely related. Taxonomy, the scientific classification of organisms, groups animals according to increasing physical, behavioral, and genetic similarity. *Species* is the most specific category, and it refers to a group of animals that will interbreed in the wild. From here, the categories get larger and less specific as the characteristics that are used to group the animals together become broader. The next, more general category after the species is the genus (the plural is genera), then comes the family, then the order, the class, and finally the phylum. The smallest category that is common to all of the birds known as eagles is the Accipitridae family, which also includes hawks, kites, and old-world vultures.

Since eagles are not closely related, it is not surprising that there is such variety among them. The smallest eagle, an Ayres' hawk-eagle from the tropical forests of Africa, may weigh as little as one and a half pounds (680g) and is slightly smaller than the common crow, while the largest species, the Stellar's sea eagle and the harpy eagle, can weigh up to twenty pounds (9kg). The North American bald and golden eagles may weigh up to fifteen pounds (6.8kg). Females are also almost always larger than males. They may be up to one-third larger, in both size and weight.

Eagles can sport many colors of plumage, including black, gray, brown, and white. Some, like the golden eagle, have several shades of brown, but many others display a plumage of brown mixed with splotches and bars of white. And a few have crests—feathers on the top of the head that are raised and lowered as part of the birds' communication system. A raised crest indicates alertness and aggression and makes the bird appear larger, while a flattened crest may indicate subordination. Crests are often raised as a part of courtship.

Wing shape varies with the flight type of the eagle. Long, broad wings, such as those on a bald eagle, are good for gliding. These wings can lift an eagle high into the sky with little effort because the bird makes excellent use of thermal updrafts. More agile species have narrower and sometimes shorter wings that allow them to dart quickly.

Eagles are excellent fliers: they have been known to fly up almost three miles (5km) into the sky. From such a great height the eagle is able to swoop down upon its prey with incredible speed, sometimes exceeding fifty miles per hour (80kph) in a power dive. Many eagles in the tropics can maneuver through the treetops with amazing agility as they chase and attack their prey at forty to fifty miles per hour (64 to 80kph).

Depending on habitat and prey species, different eagles can specialize in different types of hunting. Many eagles use a technique called perch-hunting: the eagle sits very still until it sights its prey, then it dashes out to take the prey from the ground, a tree, or a nearby source of water. Some, such as the lesser spotted eagle and the steppe eagle, actually walk for long periods in search of prey, while others slowly soar or hover over open country to detect inconspicuous prey.

An eagle's vision is excellent—some claim that it is as much as seven times more acute than a human's. Eagles' eyes are enormous relative to the size of their heads. In fact, some of the large eagles have eyes

Few animals elicit such strong emotions as the bald eagle. Although it seems an obvious choice to symbolize the United States, the bald eagle almost lost the position as national symbol to the wild turkey. This portrait makes it clear why the bald eagle won—could a turkey ever look as majestic and powerful?

almost as big as a human's, even though their heads are much smaller than ours. The position of the eyes allows the birds to see to each side, while at the same time giving them excellent binocular vision to the front. The eyes each have a translucent third eyelid called a nictitating membrane, which protects the eyes and keeps them moist.

Eagles sit at the top of the food chain. This makes them more vulnerable to the toxic chemicals in the environment, since each link of the food chain tends to concentrate chemicals from the link below. Because they are at the top of the food chain, eagles also need an extremely large area to support themselves. Generally, because of their size, they have very few enemies. Most of them take three to five years to become sexually mature, and when they do nest they may raise only one or two young each year. Most eagle mortality takes place during the first year, especially during the nestling period. Eaglets are vulnerable to nest predation and nest parasites, and if parents can't find enough food or if older siblings grab the food first, the youngest may starve. Young birds that do survive are dependent on their parents for a long time, sometimes over a year, since it takes practice to perfect hunting skills.

With their power, beauty, and strength, eagles have been considered a symbol of greatness by many different cultures throughout history. This book is a celebration in words and pictures of the glory of these majestic birds. It will showcase America's national symbol—the indigenous bald eagle—as well as some of the other beautiful birds known as eagles.

ABOVE: Eagle wings are built for soaring and gliding at slow speeds while searching for prey. The primary wing feathers narrow towards the tip. When an eagle pushes its wings down, against the air, during flight, pressure causes neighboring feathers to separate and create a series of slots. In this configuration, each feather acts like a tiny, separate airfoil, increasing the total lifting power of the wing. You can see the slots at the tip of this bald eagle's wings.

OPPOSITE: Bald eagles fish for a living and are always found near water. This bird from Alaska has found a convenient, if chilly, place to spot its next meal. An eagle's feet are more resistant to cold than a human's because they are mostly tendon and because blood vessels are arranged to keep heat from leaving the body.

ABOVE: Like other birds, black eagles have bodies adapted for flight. Their bones are hollow and may contain extensions of the lungs, called air sacs. The breast bone extends out as a deep keel, where the strong flight muscles attach. This bird's wings and muscles resist the force of gravity as it comes in for a landing.
OPPOSITE: The African fish eagle, like all eagles, uses its feet to catch and kill its prey. Once caught, the meal is carried off to a comfortable spot. Fish eagles specialize in fish, but their diet may contain many other kinds of food, including birds, mammals, and reptiles.

The ancient Roman name for the golden eagle, *Aquila,* gave rise to the English word "eagle." Golden feathers on the back of the neck of adult birds account for the English name.

Bald eagles often migrate along mountain ridges, where updrafts provide much of the energy needed for soaring and gliding. Eagles have heavy bodies relative to their wing size, so flapping flight is strenuous and birds soar when they can. An eagle soaring over the mountains is a thrilling sight.

EAGLES AROUND THE WORLD

CHAPTER

1

EAGLES ARE FOUND ON ALL OF THE WORLD'S CONTINENTS EXCEPT ANTARTICA. ALTHOUGH THEY ARE NOT, IN MANY RESPECTS, CLOSELY related to each other, there are about fifty-five species of birds that have the word "eagle" in the common name. They are classified in different genera because their physical and genetic characteristics are not similar enough to be classified together, yet there are some things that all eagles have in common with each other, as well as with other birds of prey. Eagle's bills are short and heavy, with a hooked tip and flat sides. They have short, strong feet, and the long toes have very sharp, curved talons. Their bodies are compact and powerful, with a wide breast. Eagles lay eggs several days apart and start incubating with the first egg, so the last chick to hatch is considerably smaller than the first, and has the least chance of surviv-

The white-bellied sea eagle, found on the coasts of Australia, India, and Southeast Asia, may scavenge the tide line for edibles, in addition to hunting live prey like fruit bats, gulls, sea snakes, and fish. These birds often place their nests on the cliffs of off-shore islands, where few predators threaten eggs or chicks.

ing. Even if it is not killed by an older sibling, the youngest may die of hunger because it is smaller and can't compete successfully for food.

The eagle species are divided into four general sub-groups of the Accipitridae family. Booted (or "true") eagles have feathers down their legs to their toes. Serpent eagles prey on reptiles, and are found only in the Old World. Harpies are huge eagles with long tails, and they inhabit the tropical rain forests of the Philippines, New Guinea, and South America. Sea and fish eagles have scaled, rough feet to help them catch their slippery prey, and are found near coastal and inland waters throughout the world.

Although we have good information about a number of the species, others are so solitary that very little is known about their life habits.

BOOTED EAGLES

Golden eagles are in the booted eagle group. *Aquila* was the name given to the golden eagle by the ancient Romans. Scientists have kept this Latin word for the whole genus of eagles to which the golden eagle belongs. There are several other genera of booted eagles, including *Spizaetus,* which are small crested African eagles, and *Hieraetus,* which are long-winged Old World hawk eagles. *Aquila* eagles hunt in the open country, since they need an area clear of trees

OPPOSITE: While some species of eagle are found only in very small parts of the world, the golden eagle is distributed across half the globe. Probably known to more people than any other eagle, the golden is sometimes called the King of Birds. Its image has been used by many cultures as a symbol of power and royalty.

ABOVE: Learning to come in for a landing is harder than learning to fly, and young eagles often crash at first. The wings of this Verreux's eagle show the powerful braking force needed to reach the ground under full control. This species is famous for spectacular flight displays, used in courtship and to defend nest territories.

or other obstacles in order to fly low in search of their prey.

Booted eagles can range in size, from a fairly small three-and-a-half pound (1.5kg) male eagle in the *Hieraetus* genus, to a medium-sized ten pound (4.5kg) female of the *Aquila* genus. All of these eagles have legs feathered to their toes. The larger species have heavy and powerful bills, legs, and talons, while the smaller species have slightly weaker legs and bills. The coloring of the plumage changes with age. Young booted eagles often have light and dark streaks, but as they get older their feathers darken and the streaks disappear. Mature eagles often have patches of white among the darker feathers.

The different members of this genus vary in size and strength, depending on their feeding habits. One of the largest and most powerful is the black eagle of Africa, which rarely feeds on carrion, generally killing its prey instead. As with other eagles, it is not uncommon for an older sibling to kill a younger one, so that only one eaglet is fledged from each nest. The weakest member of this genus is the lesser spotted eagle of India. This eagle prefers live food, especially small vertebrates and insects. It often practices a behavior called "kleptoparasitism," which involves harassing another bird and stealing its prey.

The genus *Hieraetus,* found in Eurasia and Australia, contains small to medium-size eagles. Again, the six species of this genus vary in size and strength. They generally live in lightly forested country and rarely feed on carrion. These eagles practice several styles of hunting, including catching smaller birds in flight, and dashing, where the eagle darts down from a perch or from soaring flight to catch an animal on the ground. They are sometimes listed as

OPPOSITE: The tawny eagle is found throughout Africa and India, except in the densest forest and the most open desert. They may spot prey, such as lizards or guineafowl, from a perch or from the air. This species also will seek food, usually carrion, by walking on the ground. They are bold thieves: they will take food from other birds of prey, storks, and ground hornbills.

ABOVE: Most Wahlberg's eagles breed in Africa, south of the equator. The nest is usually in a tall tree and may be used several years in a row. Usually a single egg is laid and with luck, one chick is reared. After nesting, the birds fly to wintering areas north of the equator.

members of the *Aquila* genus, but are generally smaller, with more slender forms, slender legs, small bills, and deeper notches in the primary wing feathers, which help them fly in wooded areas. They are very fast fliers and excellent hunters.

The genus *Spizastur* contains only one species, the black-and-white hawk eagle of Central and South America. This eagle is rather small, generally weighing around two pounds (.9kg). It is similar to *Hieraetus,* but its young are like the adults, with less sharply notched primaries. It is black with a white belly and head. The female is usually much larger than the male. The legs are feathered and the toes and talons are long, slender, and very curved. The black and white hawk eagle lives in a wide range of habitats, and hunts by dashing from a soaring flight high above the trees to catch its prey. It eats various mammals, reptiles, and birds, and has been known to attack troops of small monkeys.

The genus *Lophoaetus* also has only one species, the rather small long-crested eagle of sub-Saharan Africa. This bird has a broad tail and wings and practices dashing when it hunts. It eats mostly rodents, but will also prey on small birds or reptiles, and occasionally on insects. Both young and adults are black with a very long occipital crest composed of about six feathers.

The largest number of species in this group of eagles are in the genus *Spizaetus,* which are found in Africa, Asia, and Central and South

ABOVE LEFT: Long-crested eagles, from sub-Saharan Africa, use their crests to communicate mood and intention. A raised crest may signal alertness, interest, or aggression, while a flattened crest can indicate submission or fear. The crest may also signal a bird's species to other birds, from a distance.
ABOVE RIGHT: The martial eagle is the largest African eagle. Martial eagles are birds of the air, usually found aloft, soaring high in search of prey. Adult birds do not wander or migrate, but spend the year in their home range, which includes the nesting territory.
OPPOSITE: Young martial eagles keep their grey and white plumage, with little change from molt to molt, for about five years. At this point, as they reach sexual maturity, they quickly molt into the brown and white pattern of adults.

America. Several of these species have been used for falconry throughout the centuries. They are very fast fliers and prefer dark forests, where they can hide in the trees and surprise or ambush their prey quite easily. They have short wings for rapid flight and long tails for maneuvering easily through the trees. Some species have a bushy crest, while others have a long pointed crest, and still others have no crest at all. Their talons are long and very sharp. The adult plumage is typically barred with a very intricate color pattern, while the immature eagles have a simpler pattern.

The genus *Stephanoaetus* contains only one species, the African crowned eagle, also called the crowned hawk eagle. This is possibly the most powerful African bird of prey. It is a large and powerful eagle, and can weigh up to nine pounds (4kg). It kills monkeys and is so strong that it can carry its prey almost vertically into the air. Its hunting territory is approximately four to ten square miles (10 to 26 sq km) of tropical forest. The African crowned eagle has a heavily compressed bill, large feathered legs with short, heavy toes, and very large talons. The young have a white belly and head, while the adults are richly barred below and have a full divided crest on the top of the head.

The genus *Polemaetus* also contains only one species, the large martial eagle of Africa. Long, rather pointed wings and a short tail distinguish this bird. It has a large and somewhat compressed bill. Its legs are feathered, and the toes are long with curved talons. The immature martial eagles have a white head and white underparts, while the adults display a dark gray-brown throat and chest and an abdomen speckled with black. These birds have a short full crest, which is not always visible. They prey on monkeys, rock hyraxes, and small antelope. With a wingspan reaching eight feet (2.5m), the martial eagle has even been known to kill thirty-five-pound (16kg) bushbucks.

The last genus of this group, *Ictinaetus*, also contains only one species—the Indian black eagle, found in Asia and the East Indies. Large but lightly built, its habits are more like those of a kite, and it is often considered to be an eagle-like kite. It has very long wings and a long tail. Its talons are long and only slightly curved. The outer toes are quite short, designed for picking nestling birds from treetop nests. The feathers of the crown are pointed, forming a very slight crest. Adults are blackish, while the young are buff-colored.

SERPENT EAGLES

The second group of eagles are the serpent or snake eagles, which are found in Europe, Asia, and Africa. These small to medium-size eagles have very long, broad, pointed wings. Their toes are short, thick, and powerful, with the strength to immobilize their prey quickly. Serpent eagles hunt by hovering over open or lightly forested land, so that they can discern small, easily hidden prey. They rely on speed to catch their prey, dropping quickly out of the sky to disable the snake by crushing its skull. They swallow prey head first, but often take flight with the snake only partly swallowed, especially if they are taking it back to the nest. Since serpent eagles are susceptible to snake venom, their legs and toes are very heavily scaled to deflect the bites of snakes and other reptiles, which form their principal food.

These eagles are solitary in their habits, so we know little about them. Most of them live in the tropics, where they can easily find serpents

Largest of the snake-eagles, this brown snake-eagle shows the large, cowled head typical of this group. This bird hunts large, venomous cobras and puff adders, as well as nonpoisonous snakes. The eagle's powerful feet grip a snake's body and the reptile is disabled by bites to the spine. Snakes are swallowed head first. Scales and skin are regurgitated, after the rest is digested.

or snakes as they soar over the plains and marshes. There are six species in the genus *Circaetus*, all of which are found in sub-Saharan Africa, although the short-toed snake eagle is also found in Europe and India. Serpent eagles do not have a crest, but they do have especially large heads with yellow eyes.

The bateleur eagle is probably the best known of any of the snake eagles. This eagle is found throughout the plains and savanna woodlands of both East and West Africa. The bateleur eagle has remarkably long wings and a very short tail, and its body is rather chunky. It has black and chestnut brown plumage and a featherless, bright red face. It has been nicknamed "the flying wing" because its very short tail, which is scarcely visible when in flight, allows the bird to perform acrobatic tumbles in the air.

HARPY EAGLES

The third group, the harpy eagles, are the largest and generally the most powerful of the eagles and are found in the Americas, New Guinea, and the Philippines. These eagles are closely related to buzzards, as are the booted eagles. In general, they prey on large mammals, including monkeys.

There are four so-called "great eagles" in this group: the harpy eagle, the Philippine eagle (also called the monkey-eating eagle), the New Guinea harpy eagle, and the Guiana harpy eagle. Of these four, the best known is the harpy eagle, the only species in the genus *Harpia*. This eagle inhabits unbroken tracts of

ABOVE: Never common, the extraordinary Philippine eagle has almost disappeared, along with the tropical forest on which it depends. It is one of the largest eagles: females can weigh nearly eighteen pounds (8kg). The single chick remains with its parents for over a year, learning to find and catch flying lemurs, snakes, flying squirrels, birds, and bats.

OPPOSITE: Few birds outside mythology can match the power of the harpy eagle, one of the world's most massive birds of prey. Found in the lowland tropical forests of Central and South America, this bird is adept in flight, in spite of its size. Patrolling dense forest, harpy eagles prey on adult monkeys, porcupines, young deer, and sloths, as well as birds and reptiles.

lowland tropical forest in Central and South America. It rarely, if ever, soars; instead it takes short flights from perch to perch as it locates prey. Since the harpy eagle's habitat makes visibility difficult, this species has developed acute hearing, and hunting flights are stimulated by calls of monkeys or parrots in the bird's immediate area.

The harpy eagle is the largest eagle and possibly the most powerful bird in the world. It has the heaviest, stoutest legs of any bird of prey. In fact, a female's lower legs may be as large in diameter as a child's wrist. The toes can span nine inches (23cm), and there are some reports of talons up to five inches long (12.5cm), though they are not as sharp as those of the booted eagles. Harpy eagles have rounded, broad wings, a long tail, and a divided, two-part crest. The females are much larger than the males and may weigh up to twenty pounds (9kg). Females hunt larger prey than males—in fact, they can kill animals that are up to four times larger than those the males hunt. For example, a female harpy can kill an animal that weighs up to twenty pounds (9kg), which is sometimes as much as she weighs herself, although she cannot carry the prey whole and must tear it into smaller pieces to transport it. A male harpy can kill animals that weigh up to five pounds (2.3kg). Both males and females feed on animals such as monkeys, sloths, and opossums.

Males and females have separate hunting territories outside of the breeding season, but when the females are nesting the males bring prey for them and the young. Nests are built in the tops of the tallest trees available, and can be as high as 225 feet (68.5m) in the air. Juveniles remain close to the nest for at least a year, so adults only reproduce every three years.

Many birds of prey, including the four species of harpy eagles, sunbathe. Although scientists are not certain why they do this, it is thought that the sun helps provide vitamin D and kills parasites. Harpies sunbathe on high perches above the vegetation, waiting for a chance to hunt.

The Philippine eagle fills a niche similar to the harpy eagle, but its range is restricted to the Philippines. This species is extremely endangered (probably less than 200 remain) because logging has destroyed virtually all available habitat. There have been observations of cooperative hunting by a pair of these birds: one distracts a troop of monkeys, which allows the other to sneak up from behind and attack. This eagle has a facial ruff, which may help it locate prey by sound. This bird was known until recently as the monkey-eating eagle, although the most important prey item for this species is the flying lemur.

The New Guinea harpy eagle is also a lowland forest species, preying on mammals such as tree kangaroos and cloud rats. These birds hunt by swooping from perch to perch, and they have been known to pursue prey by chasing it along the ground. New Guinea harpies sometimes clamber about in trees, striking nests with their wings or tearing them apart with their feet to find prey. This species has a small range and a low reproductive rate, and this combined with local deforestation and the fact that they are hunted for their plumes makes them vulnerable to extinction.

The Guiana harpy eagle inhabits lowland tropical and subtropical forest, from Central America through northern Argentina. Its distribution overlaps that of the harpy, but its smaller size and partial specialization on snakes allow the birds to share habitats.

SEA EAGLES

The fourth group are the fish or sea eagles, the best known of which is the bald eagle. These eagles all live near large bodies of water and feed mainly on fish and waterfowl. They have short, bare feet and legs—that is, they have scales instead of feathers on their lower legs and toes. The scales on the bottom of their toes have tiny spicules, or spikes, which help them catch and hold slippery fish. These scales are like reptile scales in that they develop from buds or follicles, as do feathers. Some of the species in this group appear to be very closely related to vultures. The Stellar's sea eagle of Siberia and the European sea eagle are the largest members of this group, while the smallest is the lesser fishing eagle from the forests of the Far East.

African fish eagles are among the best-studied birds of prey. It has been estimated that a single bird needs to eat about half a pound (.23kg) of fish a day. Deep, clear waters are favored for fishing, as are the bases of rapids or waterfalls, where fish may be made vulnerable by turbulent water. While fish are a preferred food, these birds also take other prey, especially water birds. They have even been reported to kill adult flamingos.

The genus *Haliaeetus* contains eight species, including the bald eagle. Sea eagles can be found on almost every continent. These birds range in size from four pounds (1.8kg) to twenty pounds (9kg). They have long, broad wings and short to medium tails, which may be rounded or even wedge-shaped. Their bills are large, strong, and slightly compressed. The legs are rather short but the toes and talons are powerful. Adults generally have a bold color pattern, while the young are more uniformly and dully colored. Sea eagles are good fishers, but will also feed on mammals, birds, and carrion.

The Stellar's sea eagle is the largest of this group, weighing up to twenty pounds (9kg).

The species name of the African fish eagle is *vocifer,* and the birds are famous for their call. This is generally described as either a loud, clear series of yelps, or a loud, ringing yelp, which is uttered with the head thrown back; male and female often call in duet. Young birds make only a hoarse, cracked version of the call until they are three or four years of age.

They inhabit the coasts and river valleys of Japan, Korea, and the West Bering Sea. They live principally on Pacific salmon, which they hunt from a perch. When a fish nears the surface of the water, the Stellar's sea eagle swoops down from its perch and picks it out of the water.

The genus *Gypohierax* contains only one species—the vulturine fish eagle, also called the palm-nut vulture. This eagle does eat fish and crabs as well as small vertebrates, but the major part of its diet is palm fruit. This small eagle has long, broad wings and a short, rounded tail. Its bill is large but slightly compressed, and its talons are small but curved and sharp. Like a vulture, it has featherless, red facial skin. Its nape feathers are shaped slightly like a lance head. The adults are very striking with a white body, black wings, and a black tail band. The young may be various shades of brown.

The genus *Ichthyophaga* contains two species, which can be found from India to Southeast Asia. These are the medium-size gray-headed fishing eagle and the small lesser fishing eagle. Both have short, blunt wings and broad tails. In addition to the spicules on the bottoms of their toes, they have long, slender, strongly curved, acute talons, which aid in the capture of slippery fish. The lesser sea eagle feeds entirely on live fish that it captures, while the gray-headed eagle will also eat dead fish and some mammals. The adults display a bold brown and white pattern, while the young are much paler, mottled, and streaked.

Sea eagles, also called fish eagles, have rough skin similar to sandpaper on the bottom of their feet, which helps keep fish from slipping from their grasp. In a relaxed position, a bird's foot is closed and must be purposely opened. This is why sleeping birds don't fall off their perches, and it means that hanging onto a fish in flight is automatic. This white-bellied sea eagle shows typical aerial fishing behavior—these birds seldom actually enter the water after prey.

THE BALD EAGLE

CHAPTER
2

OF THE ELEVEN SPECIES OF SEA EAGLES LIVING THROUGHOUT THE WORLD, THE BALD EAGLE IS THE ONLY ONE INDIGENOUS TO NORTH AMERICA. It can be found from Alaska to Florida and from Mexico to Nova Scotia. We know of important nesting areas in Michigan, Wisconsin, Minnesota, Washington, Oregon, Florida, Maine, and Alaska. And a number of other states, including Tennessee, Illinois, Missouri, New York, and Pennsylvania, have many pairs nesting within their boundaries.

The major wintering areas for the bald eagle include the states bordering the Mississippi River and the states along the East and West Coasts. Depending on food availability, hundreds of bald eagles may congregate at these wintering areas. Some winter fish kills of gizzard shad along the Mississippi River have attracted as

Many eagle species, among them the bald eagle, have dramatic aerial displays that are used in courtship and territorial defense. This display, involving a spinning descent with locked talons, may be a form of ritualized combat. Other flight displays include pursuit flights, undulating "sky dancing," and a "fly-around" display.

many as four hundred to five hundred bald eagles at the same time. The densest concentrations of bald eagles are in Alaska and British Columbia, which combined may have a population of 50,000 or more bald eagles.

Forty to fifty years ago the bald eagle was believed to be made up of two distinct subspecies—the southern bald eagle, thought to begin nesting in December and January, and the northern bald eagle, believed to start nesting in March and April. Since then the bald eagle numbers have increased, and the eagles have moved back into other sections of the nation where for some years they had been almost absent.

When the bald eagle population was at its lowest point in the early 1960s, the "southern" bald eagle was concentrated primarily in Florida, away from human populations. But as Florida's bald eagle population has rebounded and its human population has increased, the bald eagles have been forced to live closer and closer to humans. Now we find bald eagles in Florida nesting in large trees in backyards, along highways, and even in school yards where children play every day.

The birds are expanding their nesting ranges and are returning to historic nesting areas. They can now be found nesting almost everywhere along the Mississippi River and its tributaries, from the Gulf of Mexico all the way north to its beginnings in Minnesota. Every year most states in the nation report more bald eagle nests than they had the previous year.

By studying these eagles we have learned that the time of nesting is based almost entirely on the location, and that there is a gradual gradient from one time to the other. In fact, the "northern" bald eagles will fly south into the southern United States and even into Mexico,

OPPOSITE: Bald eagles are tolerent of very cold temperatures. Their skin is protected by a feather cloak, lined with warm down. Feet are mostly tendon and therefore cold resistant, and the outside structure of the bill is mostly nonliving material, with little blood supply. This bird may not even know that an icicle at the tip of its bill is threatening its dignity.

ABOVE: To control their flight and respond to changes in air conditions, eagles can manipulate the shape and size of their wings, as well as the angle at which wings and even individual feathers meet the wind. While soaring, wings can be fanned open for more lift or pulled back towards the body to start a dive. This bird shows the flat wing angle typical of soaring eagles.

and the "southern" bald eagles will fly north as far as Canada. Because of these findings, the subspecies status of the bald eagle has been dropped from the literature.

The bald eagle is one of the largest of the sea eagles, second in size only to the Stellar's sea eagle. The female is larger than the male: it stands approximately thirty inches (76cm) high, has a wingspan of five to eight feet (1.5 to 2.5m), and weighs ten to fourteen pounds (4.5 to 6.5kg). Males are generally half the weight of females, although their wingspans are not much smaller. It takes at least four years for a bald eagle to become sexually mature, during which time its dark brown plumage gradually changes to the adult plumage: a white tail and a white head with a golden beak.

Bald eagles are generally found near lakes and rivers that are well stocked with fish, which are their primary food source. They are able to fish through the winter because their legs and feet are free of feathers, so water washes right off their legs without freezing. Unlike the osprey, or fish hawk, the bald eagle does not dive into the water to capture fish. Instead, it dips its feet into the water and catches its prey close to the surface. Only the bald eagle's feet get wet, unless the fish is so large that the eagle cannot lift it from the water, which sometimes happens with salmon in the northwestern part of North America. When the eagle has captured such a large fish, it may try to drag it to shore. If the bird tires while struggling, it may need to dip deeper into the water.

If there are no or few fish available, bald eagles are not averse to feeding on carrion. And in the northern areas, where the waters freeze over during the winter, bald eagles rely on hunting other prey, such as ducks.

A SYMBOL OF FREEDOM

The bald eagle was selected as the symbol of the United States in 1782. The choice was between the image of a bald eagle and that of a male turkey, with its broad tail spread open and strutting through the open woods. We know that Ben Franklin preferred the strutting turkey over the bald eagle. He felt that the eagle was cowardly and "of bad moral character." Apparently he had witnessed a few too many bald eagles stealing food from other birds. But those who backed the bald eagle won out, and more than two hundred years later, many people still feel that there is nothing like a bald eagle soaring above us to really symbolize freedom.

ABOVE: This is the official seal of the United States of America.

OPPOSITE: The bald eagle's white head gave rise to its English name, although the bird has a full head of feathers. It is often thought that the name came about because, seen from a distance, the white feathers make the head look naked. In fact, however, the word "bald" also means streaked or marked with white, and it is this that gave the bird its name.

NESTING

It is believed that bald eagles mate for life. But if one member of a pair should die or leave the area for some reason, the other will take a new mate whenever possible. Bald eagles are as faithful to their nests as they are to their mates: a pair will probably use the same nest every year until one dies.

During the nesting season, eagles are quite territorial and will keep other eagles out of their own nesting area. Interestingly, one scientist in Canada documented that a female eagle will drive other females out of her territory, while a male will allow females to enter. Similarly, a male eagle will drive out other males, while a female will let them stay. This gender defense mechanism helps preserve a pair's fidelity. For those that have lost a mate, wandering unpaired birds may be the key to finding another mate.

The success of a nesting territory depends on certain conditions being met. Since fish is the major diet of the bald eagle, the nest must be close to a good source of fish. The most suc-

OPPOSITE: Like other fish eagles, bald eagles often sit on favorite perches, with a good view of a stream or lake, waiting for fish to appear near the surface. It takes only seconds for an eagle to launch itself, glide to the water, pluck out a meal, and sail away. Unlike the osprey, a fishing bird that often plunges underwater after prey, bald eagles seldom get wet while seeking a meal.

ABOVE: Eagles often incorporate aromatic leaves into their nests. These act as a natural insecticide, helping to keep the nest free of mites, fleas, and other pests. This is especially important for species that use the same nests from year to year, as insects can survive from one season to the next.

cessful nests are built within one mile (1.6km) of a major body of water. If a pair of eagles builds its nest farther away from the water source, they may go through all of the motions of nest building, egg laying, incubation, and even trying to raise their young, but to no avail. If they are unable to find adequate food, the young will never fledge.

An aerie, or nest, is usually found in the crown of a large tree, although in Arizona many of the nests are found on ledges high on rocky cliff sides. The birds generally choose a tree that is taller than the rest so that they can look out over the tops of the other trees. These single tall trees are harder for predators to approach without being seen. They may also choose such high perchs because adult eagles need open space to jump as they leave the nest. Because of its size and weight, it is very difficult for a bald eagle to just take off and climb rapidly into the air. It must attain a certain speed or momentum before it is able to ascend quickly. Normally, when a bald eagle leaves a nest or perch, it will drop down and then pull back up as it gains the speed it needs to remain airborne.

A pair of bald eagles may have one, two, or even three nests within their breeding territory. A new nest, which can be built in just a few weeks, may measure four feet (1.2m) high and six feet (1.8m) across at the top. Many pairs will use the same nest year after year, simply adding new material to it. These older nests can reach a width of up to nine feet (2.7m) and weigh more than two tons (1.8t). Other pairs have several nests and rotate from one nest to another each year.

Bald eagles select tall trees, emerging high above surrounding woods, as sites for their nests. Branches and sticks are used to create a platform, exposed to the wind but safe from predators. The same site may be used for many years by a single pair, or by several pairs in succession, each adding to the nest when beginning the breeding cycle. Some nests have been estimated to weigh several tons.

The nest itself is usually constructed of small limbs from other trees that the eagle breaks off during flight. Three to six feet (1 to 1.8m) in length and up to two inches (5cm) in diameter, the larger limbs are carried to the nest clenched in the eagle's feet, and the smaller limbs are carried in the beak. Cottonwood, which is very brittle and can be easily broken by the eagles in flight, is frequently used in nest building. The limbs must be interwoven so that the nest will stay together even in high winds, because the nest usually sits above the surrounding trees, where it will be exposed to wind from any direction.

The materials used in nest building and the locations of nests vary depending upon the geographical area. For example, since there are no trees on the Aleutian Islands of Alaska, the eagles there build nests, made out of seaweed, on the tops of knolls. In the upper Midwest, the preferred tree is the white pine, thanks to its open crown, but eagles may use any other tree that is tall enough for its crown to reach above the nearby trees. Along the Mississippi River the preferred tree appears to be the pin oak. The nests may be anywhere from 50 to 120 feet (15 to 36.5m) above the forest floor.

A bald eagle nest is so large that when a bander wants to band the young, he or she must often climb into the nest. The young birds will back away from the bander, and if they are too old they may actually back off the far edge

ABOVE: Both members of a bald eagle pair share the work of nest building, incubation, chick brooding, and chick feeding. One bird is always on the nest after eggs are laid, while the other hunts or adds to the nest. OPPOSITE: When an eaglet hatches it is helpless, needing parents to provide both warmth and food. Adults select easily digested tidbits for tiny chicks, which beg eagerly and grow quickly.

of the nest. When this happens, the birds will then have to be rescued from the tops of the trees below, which is no easy feat. That is why eagle banders, to be successful, must band the young before they are seven or eight weeks old.

Nests sometimes become so large that the supporting limbs cannot carry the weight. Now that the bald eagle population is expanding into new areas, many nests are being built in trees that are unable to support such heavy structures. The significant size and weight also mean that the nests are vulnerable to high winds. The end result of all these situations is that the nests are more apt to fall to the ground before the young have fledged.

The platform, or top of a bald eagle nest, is basically flat or even a bit cup-shaped at the beginning of the nesting season. The center of the nest contains a slight pocket or depression, which is lined with grass, moss, and feathers. It is in this pocket that one to four eggs are laid. Like many other eagles, adult bald eagles commonly add fresh green vegetation throughout the nesting season. Eaglets have been seen eating leaves from branches built into the nest.

Over the course of the season, the center pocket of the nest gradually disappears and the nest becomes flatter. As the young eaglets grow, they jump onto the sides of the nest and practice flapping their wings, which knocks off some of the outside branches. The nest that was flat on top during the incubation of the eggs becomes more rounded just before the young are fledged.

OLD ABE

Old Abe, a young bald eagle, was the mascot for the Eighth Regiment of Wisconsin Volunteer Infantry during the Civil War. He was with the regiment as it moved through Kentucky and Tennessee after the battle of Shiloh to Corinth, where he was exposed to his first major encounter. Tales were told of Old Abe's bravery—that sometimes during a battle he would break his jesses and fly into the fray, only returning to his perch once the fighting was over. In other stories, when the shots came close, the eagle would jump off his perch and try to hide under whatever was nearby. But this more cowardly view was not the one romanticized by the press.

He was with the Wisconsin regiment as it chased Confederate generals Price, Taylor, and Forest across Arkansas, Louisiana, and Missouri and then back to Mississippi. Old Abe participated in thirty-seven engagements and was never wounded. The eagle's last engagement was at Hurricane Creek, Mississippi on August 13, 1864, when he and his Company C from Eau Claire, part of the Eagle Brigade, stormed across the creek as the Union attempted to push General Nathan Bedford Forrest back away from Memphis.

After the Civil War, Old Abe became a living symbol of the victorious Union. On September 26, 1864, Old Abe was presented to Wisconsin Governor James T. Lewis "as an honored and inspiring memento of the Eighth Regiment, and the times in which it had fought the battles of the nation." As with the tattered battle flags of the Wisconsin regiment, he became a "war relic." He was a part of many political rallies and conventions and reminded all who saw him of what the North had fought so hard to preserve.

Old Abe occupied a two-room apartment in the basement of the Wisconsin Capitol building until he died on March 26, 1881, from respiratory complications that had developed from smoke inhaled during a fire in the Capitol a month earlier. His body was mounted in a glass case and placed on display in the Capitol rotunda until 1885, when the display was moved to the War Museum, part of the State Historical Society's rooms in the Capitol. In 1903 it was moved into the G.A.R. Memorial Hall in the Capitol, where it was destroyed in 1904, when the building was consumed by fire.

The finest monument to this eagle and the men with which it went into battle was constructed at Vicksburg, where the Eighth Regiment had helped General Grant capture this Mississippi River stronghold. The monument was a fifty-seven-and-a-half-foot-tall (17.5m) granite column with a six-foot (1.8m) bronze statue of Old Abe on the top. This monument was dedicated on May 22, 1911, just forty-eight years after the grand assault actually occurred. Sadly, the original bronze eagle was damaged by lightning in 1944.

When the Allies launched their invasion of France in 1944, it was decided that Old Abe should symbolically take part in the greatest airborne assault in history. Today, eighteen thousand members of America's elite 101st Airborne Division, the "Screaming Eagles," still wear a patch depicting Old Abe on their left shoulders.

ABOVE: The patch of the 101st Airborne Division.

This pair of bald eagles doesn't mind the snow. Eagle feathers are hollow and light, yet they are extremely warm. The feathers trap layers of air to insulate the bird against icy temperatures, and the down next to the skin prevents heat from escaping.

The female usually lays two to three eggs over the course of a few days, but she and the male begin incubating the first egg almost as soon as it is laid. Incubation takes approximately thirty-five days, and the work of keeping the eggs warm is shared equally by the male and female. The chicks hatch in the order in which the eggs were laid, which means that the first laid (and thus the first hatched) egg has at least some advantage over its younger siblings.

The first hatched eaglet is automatically larger and more coordinated than its siblings because it is older and has had more time to develop, but because it is stronger and can make more noise, it continues to have the advantage. Parent birds tend to feed the loudest chick, so the younger (smaller) chicks only get what is left over.

If there is enough food available, there is little difference in the size of the chicks. However, if there is a shortage of food, the oldest and biggest chick gets the largest share of food and grows much faster than the others. Eventually, the littlest eaglet either starves or is pushed from the nest. Evolutionarily, it is better to be unfair in food distribution and have one chick live to be fully fledged than it is to be fair and have two weak or dead chicks. This is why the average production of bald eagles is less than two young per nest.

Once the eggs hatch, the parents provide food for the chicks for at least thirteen more weeks, until they can fly. In fact, it may be fourteen or fifteen weeks before the young are able to hunt successfully on their own. If there is enough food available during these weeks, the

Young bald eagles remain with their parents for several weeks after they start to fly. Learning to hunt successfully takes time and practice. Adults provide enough food to keep offspring healthy but hungry, so that they will continue to practice hunting.

young will grow so much that when they finally do leave the nest, they may be even larger than their parents. This extra weight is helpful for survival, since the young eagles may go hungry rather often until they get good at hunting.

When the eaglets first hatch, they are covered with a very soft down. The pinfeathers start to develop in approximately three weeks, and by six or seven weeks the feathers are about half grown. The feet and legs are almost fully grown at this age. By the time the young bald eaglets are ready to leave the nest, they will have a dark brown beak and a rich dark brown plumage. The white head and tail and the golden beak do not develop until the birds are four to six years old.

The beak itself is an excellent indicator of age. When an eaglet hatches, it uses its egg tooth—a pointed bump on the top of the beak—to break out of the shell. This white bump gradually disappears during the first four weeks. The gold color starts to develop at the base of the beak when the eagle is two years old and will gradually spread out over the whole beak by age five. This gold color is derived from plant pigments, which the eagles get from ingesting plant-eating prey. Since bald eagles are not born with golden beaks but acquire it from food sources, the amount of gold in the beak is helpful in determining age.

After about the ninth week, the eaglets' feathers have become quite developed. For the next two or three weeks the eaglets spend a lot of time standing on the edge of the nest and flapping their wings. Sometimes they actually lift themselves off the nest during these practices. If a strong gust of wind comes along, a young eaglet may be blown off the nest and go crashing into the treetop canopy below. When it is time for the eaglets to fly, the parents will not feed them on the nest but will coax the young birds to jump out of the nest to come for their meals. Researchers estimate that forty percent of young eaglets don't survive their first flight.

Once the young eaglets have fledged, they will hang around the nest for some time, and their parents will often bring food back for them. The young use the nest as a feeding platform for two to three weeks, until they become capable of catching their own food.

A full nesting cycle takes almost twenty weeks from the time the parents first return to a nest to repair it to the time the young are able to take care of themselves. During that five-month period the adults can usually be found somewhere in their one- to two-square-mile (2.5 to 5 sq km) territory.

The timing of the twenty-week nesting season varies dramatically depending upon the geographical area. For example, in the southern United States (from Florida to Arizona), eggs are laid in late December and January, and the young fly by the end of April. In the central part of the country (Kentucky, Tennessee, and Illinois), eggs are laid during late January and early February, and the young fly by mid-June. In northern Wisconsin, Michigan, and Minnesota, eggs are laid in March and the young fly by early July. And farther north, in Canada, eggs are laid in late April and the young fly by mid-August—just in time to head south for the winter.

MIGRATION

Once the nesting season is over, many bald eagles begin to move around. If they have been nesting or were raised in the southern part of the United States, they may move north to cooler climates. If they have been nesting or were raised in the northern part of the continent, they may move south to find open water

because the source of their summer food—the inland lakes and rivers—will soon freeze over. This is the fundamental reason for eagle migration: the birds are looking for sources of food for the winter.

Even researchers find facts about eagle migration to be elusive. Eagles are observed in one place, such as their nesting area, and then later they are seen somewhere else, such as their wintering area. But the mechanics of how they get from one location to the other—and how they recognize these locations—is still being studied.

There is an old adage that "geese fly in flocks but eagles fly alone." This is not entirely true, because the fact is that bald eagles, like geese, tend to move in groups. The theory is that these are local communities that happen to be moving in the same direction at the same time, following the same impulses, but not intentionally migrating together. A group or "stream" of migrating bald eagles may be twenty to thirty miles (32 to 48km) long. At any one spot an observer may see only one or two eagles at a time. However, if the observer can find a good vantage point where the view is unlimited for several miles in either direction, a whole line of eagles can be seen with the birds spread out so that there is one bird every half mile (805m) or so.

Eagles must hunt for a living and often defend a home range or territory against competition from other hunters. Fish are distributed differently than other prey, often moving in schools, and this allows fish-eagles to be gregarious when gathering at good fishing grounds. Scientists have speculated that birds living in groups watch each other to discover good feeding areas, and this may be true for bald eagles.

BALD EAGLE MIGRATION

The fidelity by bald eagle communities to specific migratory routes has been excellently documented by Dr. Alan Harmata. Dr. Harmata had put radio transmitters on three members of a community of wintering bald eagles out in the deserts of Colorado. When his first radio-tagged bird started north, Dr. Harmata got into a plane he had equipped with a radio receiver to follow the bird.

Dr. Harmata plotted the bird's route on a map. The bird seemed to wander as it went along this side of a lake, up that side of a valley, through that draw, down along one side of a river, along the side of another lake, and right over a ridge as it moved north up the east side of the Rockies, out of Colorado, up through Montana, and into Canada. Finally, Dr. Harmata's plane was running low on gas and he had to set it down to refuel. When he got back into the air, he could no longer pick up the radio signal, so he went back to Colorado to the bald eagle's wintering grounds.

A few days later the second bald eagle headed north, so once again Dr. Harmata jumped in his plane to follow the bird. This second eagle followed the same route as the first—along this side of a lake, up that side of a valley, and over the ridge—but just like the first time, Dr. Harmata's plane ran short of fuel and he had to stop to refuel. And again, when he got back into the air, he could not locate the radio signal.

But he still had one bird with a radio back on the wintering grounds. So he returned to Colorado to wait for his last bird to leave. In just a few days it, too, took to the air and headed north. Again, Dr. Harmata followed this third eagle as it flew exactly the same route, but this time Dr. Harmata knew the route the bird would take, so he stopped to refuel sooner than he had the first two times. When he got back into the air, he followed the same route the first two eagles had flown and—lo and behold—he caught up with the third eagle. This time he was able to follow the bird north through Canada all the way to the Great Slave Lake in the Northwest Territory. After this eagle had settled down near the lake, Dr. Harmata switched his receiver to the other radio frequencies and found his first two birds within thirty miles (48km) of this one. So it turned out that his wintering community of eagles was a nesting community of Canadian eagles that had followed the same route to get from the Colorado wintering area to the nesting area, even though the eagles migrated on different days.

Adult bald eagles, such as this one, do not migrate with juveniles. In fact, newly fledged eagles begin migration before their parents. No one knows what triggers young birds to begin their journey, or what tells them where to travel.

Bald eagles will generally follow the same route year after year. Whether different communities of birds share the same route is not known, but birds will normally be seen migrating past one location at the same spot. In some parts of the Mississippi River flyway, the migration route is just over the treetops above the bluffs on one side of the river. In other parts, it is right out in the middle of the river, but quite high. And in some locations the route is actually inland, away from the river.

While we have some understanding of adult migration patterns, we are still working on questions of fledgling eagle migration. It was not until the 1950s that we learned anything at all about the migration of young eagles. Charles Broley is credited with banding a number of young eagles and for the first time giving us evidence that young bald eagles do, in fact, make significant migrations. Some of the first birds he banded in Florida were found as far north as Ohio, in the United States, and southern

PAGES 52-53: This photograph clearly shows the open slots formed during the power stroke of an eagle's wing in flight, and the way each feather twists individually, increasing lift.

ABOVE LEFT: Eagles spend a significant amount of time resting quietly. This makes good sense, as every bit of energy expended must be acquired by hunting. According to one estimate, only one out of eighteen attacks results in a catch.

ABOVE RIGHT: An eagle's body temperature is over 102 degrees Fahrenheit (38.8°C) and keeping warm is basic to survival. Food provides energy and feathers provide insulation. An eagle's feathers weigh more than twice as much as its skeleton. Birds spend hours each day making sure each feather is clean and in its place.

Ontario, in Canada. Interestingly, the immature birds tend to migrate south earlier in the year than the adults. We don't yet understand how the young birds know where to go and which routes they must take.

Bald eagles that nest or are raised in the northern regions will start to move south at the end of August or the first part of September, and the migration continues in waves throughout January and sometimes even into February. In fact, the migration back north starts at around the end of January, so that while some populations have just arrived, others are ready to depart.

As with other bird migrations, the bald eagle migrations are affected by weather conditions. A huge winter storm may slow things up for a few days, but the birds will move on again as soon as they are able. The general dates for each wave will vary by only a few days each year.

The bald eagles of North America are the only eagles that participate in extreme migrations, but not all bald eagles fly far away. Some travel relatively short distances, and many eagles—especially those that nest in the South—actually stay in the same area throughout the year. They have no need to migrate if they have an adequate food source throughout the year.

An eagle's bill, like those of other birds, consists of a framework of bone, covered with a horn-like material that is similar to human fingernails. The bill covering grows throughout a bird's life, compensating for wearing down during use. Birds often clean or condition the bill by scraping it against a hard surface, as this bald eagle is doing. The bill is used not just for eating, but for preening the feathers and holding prey or nesting materials.

OPPOSITE: A bird's wing and a human's arm trace back to common structures in ancient animals. The section of the wing closest to the body contains the humerus, radius, and ulna, the bones that in humans form the arm between shoulder and wrist. This part of the wing provides most of the lift for flying. The second part of the wing, analagous to the human hand, is the propeller. In flight, it is control of this section that is used to manipulate speed and direction.

ABOVE: Once a bald eagle pair has formed, the two birds usually remain together until one bird dies. During the breeding season both birds help protect the nest territory against intrusion by other eagles and predators. Vocalizations are an important part of territorial defense, providing warning from a distance that an area is defended. Another function of bald eagle calls may be to reinforce the bond between male and female.

PAGES 58-59: Like most eagles, bald eagles kill prey with their feet, piercing it with razor sharp talons and crushing it with powerful toes. The bottom of the foot is rough, to help hold slippery fish. While these birds can walk on the ground, their feet are far more comfortable gripping a branch.
ABOVE: A bald eagle's tail is nearly as important as its wings, providing lift for flight and force for steering and braking. The bird pictured here is preening the feathers in its tail, running each through its bill to remove any dirt and make sure that the barbs and barbules that make up the vane of the feather are correctly aligned. The preen gland, at the base of the tail, provides oil for protecting and waterproofing.
OPPOSITE: For those expecting a clarion battle call, the bald eagle's voice can only be described as disappointing. "Shrill," "high pitched," and "twittering" are among the adjectives commonly used for bald eagle vocalizations. Like other birds, eagles lack vocal cords. Sound is produced in the syrinx, a bony chamber located where the trachea (windpipe) divides to go to the lungs.

PAGES 62-63: Bald eagles nest in very exposed sites, which protect eggs and chicks from most predators but sometimes make for uncomfortable roosting. When not nesting, eagles may use more sheltered perches to avoid bitter winds and rain.

OPPOSITE: Every part of an eagle is made for good aerodynamics. Heavy organs and muscles are centrally located, bones are hollow, and the head, wings, and tail are streamlined. When birds are not nesting, reproductive organs actually shrink, and expand again in the next cycle.

ABOVE: Bald eagles often have favorite perches. A good perch may have a clear view of a rich fishing spot, making it easy to swoop down when a fish nears the surface.

ABOVE: Bald eagles, and eagles in general, do not depend much on their sense of smell. While their vision is acute, their olfactory sense is not particularly highly developed.

OPPOSITE: Bald eagles often hunt by flying slowly along the shore of a lake or river, looking for fish, either dead or alive. Snatching a fish from near the water's surface takes great coordination. Because the bird's head moves ahead of its legs, it cannot actually see a fish at the moment of capture.

Bald eagle males are smaller than females. Adult bald eagles have wingspans ranging from under six feet (1.8m) to over eight feet (2.4m). A small male can weigh as little as six and a half pounds (2.9kg), while a large female can weigh as much as fourteen pounds (6.3kg).

Most eagles are solitary, requiring a large hunting territory to provide enough food for even a single bird. In some species, even the male and female from a pair have separate hunting zones in the nonbreeding season. Fish eagles are the exception, because their food is often concentrated, not distributed sparsely. In winter, bald eagles are often found in groups, taking advantage of a local abundance of fish.

OPPOSITE: The mottled white on this bird's belly indicates that it is a only few years old. Newly fledged bald eagles have dark bellies and heads, then molt into a blotched plumage. As adults, the belly and back are again dark, while the head is pure white. The distinct juvenile pattern, signaling that a bird is not ready to breed, may reduce aggression from territorial adults.

ABOVE: These bald eagles, perhaps two pairs and a juvenile, appear to be enjoying a quiet rest in the sun. When it comes time to hunt, this perch will provide a good view of the ocean and the fish it contains. Bald eagles fish in both fresh and salt water.

PAGES 72-73: The fossil history of birds is poor, and that of birds of prey exceptionally so. Animals with feathers had already evolved 150 million years ago. There is evidence that hawks, similar to those we see today, flew sixty million years ago, but little evidence to show their evolution from earlier forms. There is almost no information on the evolution of eagles.

ABOVE: This grouping of bald eagles shows how the birds change wing shape at different stages of the flight cycle.

OPPOSITE: A bald eagle's beak is a strong weapon, more complex than it first appears. The hooked tip is used for tearing. Just behind the hook, the upper mandible, sharp enough to slice tough skin, overlaps the lower, creating scissors. This formidable tool is also delicate enough to groom a mate's feathers or feed a morsel to a newly hatched chick.

Birds have sparse musculature on the back and well-developed ventral muscles. The main muscle of flight is the pectoralis, responsible for pulling the wing down during the power phase of the flight cycle. The muscles that raise the wing are also at the bird's front. Tendons pass through a hole in the bones of the shoulder, like a rope and pulley, to control the wing from above.

The shape of an eagle's wing and that of an airplane are similar, controlled by the same laws of physics. The upper surface of both kinds of wings is curved from front to back, and thicker at the front edge. In motion, air flows over the top and bottom wing surfaces, moving faster over the curved top. Faster air produces less pressure, so higher pressure from the air below the wing causes a net lifting force.

ABOVE: Wintering bald eagles have four different fishing techniques. Most successful is wading from shore to catch fish with the bill. They may also swoop from flight or from a perch to scoop fish from the water, or stand at the edge of floating ice to grab fish with bill or talons.

OPPOSITE: This bald eagle is enjoying the rewards of a successful hunt. Birds have no teeth, so large prey must be torn into chunks that are small enough to swallow. Digestion begins in the glandular stomach, which contains an acid that dissolves bones. Next the food passes to the gizzard. Birds such as pheasants use this organ for grinding tough plant matter, but in birds of prey, indigestible materials accumulate in the gizzard and are later regurgitated as a pellet called a cast. The diets of birds of prey are studied by picking apart casts to identify the scales, bones, or fur of the prey.

LEFT: How fast can an eagle fly? This question is harder to answer than you might expect. Eagles fly for hunting, migrating, and courtship. Like people and horses, some eagles are faster than others. Eagles soar, glide, flap, and dive, seldom, if ever, over easily measured distances. Estimating flight speed over long distances is easier than trying to time bursts of speed. During spring migration, calculations from radio tracking studies have shown flight speeds of about thirty miles an hour (48kph), maintained for hours at a time.
ABOVE: Bald eagles are fish specialists, but they also hunt and eat other kinds of prey. This provides flexibility, especially if the nearby body of water freezes. Squirrels, muskrats, rabbits, and even roadkill can be alternate food sources.

ABOVE: There is an old legend that the eagle alone among animals can gaze upon the sun. According to a translation of St. Augustine, "The sun invigorates the eyes of eagles, but injures our own."

RIGHT: Can you determine the age of a bald eagle by looking at it? During its lifetime, a bald eagle wears many different coats of feathers, and for the first few years each coat is different. Once a bird is six years old, however, it stops changing plumage patterns. An older bird might have heavier leg scales, but it is rare to see a wild eagle exhibit changes related to old age. Eagles must be in top condition to survive the challenge of daily life.

THE GOLDEN EAGLE

CHAPTER

3

THE MAGNIFICENT GOLDEN EAGLE HAS, FOR CENTURIES, BEEN CALLED THE *KING OF BIRDS*. IT WAS USED BY THE ROMANS, SYRIANS, AND EGYPTIANS to symbolize their great empires. And it is this eagle that is mentioned time and again in the Bible, where it is praised for its strength, power, and speed of flight. Boasting a wingspan of up to seven feet (2m), the females of this majestic species can weigh up to fifteen pounds (7kg). The golden eagle, with feathers all the way to its toes, is found in North America, Europe, Asia, and northern Africa.

Once common throughout North America, the golden eagle now nests primarily in the Rocky Mountains, due to the hunting and poisoning that have made survival elsewhere on the continent impossible. It has been estimated that as many as twelve thousand

The golden eagle's scientific name is *Aquila chrysaetos. Aquila* is Latin for eagle. *Chrysos* is the Greek word for golden, and *aetos* is Greek for eagle. The golden feathers on the nape of the adult bird's neck are not always obvious, especially from a distance.

of these birds may winter in Wyoming. They are scattered throughout the state, so an accurate count is impossible to achieve.

Until very recently, the golden eagle had not nested in the eastern part of North America for fifty years. The last golden eagle nest east of the Mississippi River was found on Ferry Bluff near the Wisconsin River in the 1940s. But in 1997, after a great deal of effort and years of work by various states in the Southeast, a nest was established in the mountains of Georgia.

The golden eagle is much more solitary than the bald eagle. Normally found in very remote areas away from any human settlements, the golden eagle population has declined tremendously as wilderness areas have become developed. The golden eagle never congregates in large numbers during the winter season, as the bald eagle does near its open-water feeding areas. Because of this, usually only one or two golden eagles are seen in one place at a time.

One of the world's greatest hunters, the golden eagle seldom eats carrion if it has the opportunity to hunt for itself. Its hunting territory may be quite extensive—up to 162 square miles(260 sq km)—depending on the quantity and type of food that is available. This species lives in fairly open country such as mountains or marshes, and it prefers low or sparse vegetation so that it can search for prey while it is soaring. Groundhogs, marmots, foxes, skunks, cats, rabbits, grouse, ground squirrels, crows, pheasants, meadowlarks, tortoises, and snakes are all prey. Golden eagles have been accused of taking lambs, small pigs, and other domesticated animals, but many people feel that this

OPPOSITE: Golden eagles are widely distributed throughout North America and Eurasia, as well as in North Africa. They are members of the group called the booted or "true" eagles, characterized by legs that are fully feathered down to the foot.

ABOVE: While about the same size as bald eagles, golden eagles are more powerful and specialize in preying on mammals. They have been persecuted for centuries by farmers and ranchers who are convinced that the birds are a threat to livestock, although there is little evidence that they kill sheep, goats, or cattle.

ABOVE: Golden eagles may nest at the top of tall trees, but more frequently they build at the edge of a cliff overlooking their hunting grounds. Some nests are huge; others are simple scrapes in the earth surrounded by branches. A pair of birds may have as many as ten nests in their territory, either using the same one every year or moving from one to another.

OPPOSITE: Eagles consider safety first when choosing a nest site. Adult eagles have few predators besides man, but young eagles can be a tasty meal for many creatures. This golden eagle nest, in a chalk cliff, is almost unapproachable.

activity has been exaggerated. Extensive studies have shown that young golden eagles do occasionally take very young lambs, but livestock losses due to eagles are very small compared with those that are due to poor management practices. However, there is a tendency to blame eagles for all lambs lost, and the fact that golden eagles will eat carrion, including domesticated animals that have already died, has exacerbated the problem. Farmers and ranchers have shot and poisoned golden eagles throughout the West to prevent them from preying on livestock. In fact, Texas even had a bounty on eagles not many years ago. If food is scarce, a pair of golden eagles may drive any other golden eagles and predators out of their nesting territory to insure an adequate food supply for themselves and their young.

NESTING

Like other large eagles, golden eagles build fairly sizable nests and use them year after year. These eagles usually nest on cliffs in the mountains, but they have been known to nest in large

EAGLES IN THE BIBLE

There are many references to eagles in the Bible, and it is believed that the references are specifically about the golden eagle because it is the largest eagle in northern Africa.

The Lord shall bring a nation against thee from far, from the end of the earth, as swift as the eagle flieth; a nation whose tongue thou shalt not understand.
—Deuteronomy 28:49

Then I looked and I heard an eagle crying with a loud voice, as it flew in mid-heaven, 'woe, woe, woe to those who dwell upon the earth.'
—Revelation 8:13

Doth the eagle mount up at thy command, and make her nest on high? She dwelleth and abideth on the rock, upon the crag of the rock, and the strong place.
—Job 39:27–28

Who satisfieth thy mouth with good things; so that thy youth is renewed like the eagle's.
—Psalms 103:5

Wilt thou set thine eyes upon that which is not? For riches certainly make themselves wings; they fly away as an eagle toward heaven.
—Proverbs 23:4–5

But they that wait upon the Lord shall renew their strength; they shall mount up with wings as eagles; they shall run, and not be weary; and they shall walk, and not faint.
—Isaiah 40:31

For thus saith the Lord; Behold, he shall fly as an eagle, and shall spread his wings over Moab.
—Jeremiah 48:40

Our persecutors are swifter than the eagles of the heaven: they pursued us upon the mountains, they laid wait for us in the wilderness.
—Lamentations 4:19

OPPOSITE: A golden eaglet, only a few weeks old, crouches in response to a possible threat. Dark feathers are beginning to replace the pale down.
ABOVE: Golden eagles may lay as many as three eggs, but the usual number is two. These youngsters are about two months old. Most of their feathers have grown in, but it will still be several weeks before they are ready to leave the nest.

trees in the plains. Early pioneers found golden eagles nesting in the large cottonwood trees that were scattered across the western plains.

First-year golden eagle nests may be as small as three feet (1m) in diameter and eighteen inches (46cm) high, but in just a year or so the eagle pair will add materials until they are up to six feet (1.8m) across and seven feet (2m) high. These nests may be located from ten to a hundred feet (3 to 30m) above the ground. When sitting on their nests, the adult birds generally have a very commanding view of the natural world around them.

The nests are made of large sticks up to two inches (5cm) in diameter and six feet (1.8m) in length. The material in the lining of the nest cavity varies depending on the eagles and what is available in the immediate vicinity. In some cases eagles have used pepper and eucalyptus tree leaves for the lining, brought in from several miles away. The kestrel and the western kingbird have been known to nest in the sides of golden eagle nests—even while the eagles are using the top of the structure.

It does not take long for eagles to build a nest. In fact, in 1930, one eagle was observed bringing seven sticks to its nest in a matter of just ten minutes. The same nest may be used for many years, but normally the birds have several in their nesting territory that they use alternately during succeeding years.

Most females lay two eggs, although sometimes they lay one egg, and occasionally they lay three. There have been one or two reports of four eggs being recovered from a golden eagle nest, but there are no reports of four young

ABOVE: Feathers, like hair, are nonliving structures produced by groups of skin cells called follicles. Feathers consist of interlocking microscopic structures that are light but very strong. Layers of feathers trap air to insulate birds against cold and protect them from rain.

OPPOSITE: While both members of a bald eagle pair take equal turns at incubating eggs, with golden eagles the female does the majority and often all incubation and brooding. The male hunts and brings back food for the female and, after they hatch, for chicks. Pairs often take a year off between nesting attempts.

ever being fledged from a nest. Varying in color from dull white to buff cream or pinkish white, the eggs have brown or drab speckles and splotches scattered over their surfaces. From year to year, the color and shading of all the eggs from one female tend to be very similar. The size of the eggs may vary from two and a half to three and a half inches (67 to 89mm) in length and from two to two and a half inches (49 to 66mm) in width.

The male golden eagle usually does not share in the incubation of the eggs, although some males do incubate as much as females. The male does bring food to the female while she is sitting on the eggs. Incubation time varies from forty-one days to the more common forty-five days. During that time the female, who is very loyal to her eggs, will remain in the nest unless extremely disturbed. Climbers have been able to almost touch a female before she would leave the nest. If the female is driven from the nest when she is sitting on eggs, she often does not return, although if she leaves chicks in the nest she will certainly come back. She may desert her eggs but never her young.

The young eaglets stay in the nest for nine to eleven weeks before they fledge. While in the nest the young eagles' plumage goes through three different stages. For the first three to four weeks the birds are downy. During the next three to four weeks the feathers are growing. By the last three weeks the young birds are fully

ABOVE: Young eagles practice flight in the nest, but this helps them develop muscles more than coordination. It takes time to learn to control flight and especially landing. This eaglet will soon try again.
OPPOSITE: The golden feathers on the nape that give the golden eagle its name are shown here very clearly. The size and location of the gold patch vary slightly in golden eagle populations on different continents.

feathered, and they spend a great deal of time flapping their wings to develop the strength they will need to fly. They remain in the nesting territory for about three months while their parents teach them how to hunt on their own.

The young eaglets retain their first coat of juvenile feathers for one year before they grow new feathers. The fresh plumage is darker and the crown and hackles are darker and less golden than that of the adults. Two-thirds of the young golden eagle's tail is white at the base, while the outer third is brownish black. At first there is a very narrow white band on the tip of the tail, but this wears off during the first year. When flying, the young golden eagle appears to have a wide, dark band at the end of its tail. As the eagle grows, the amount of white in the tail

Doris Mager, the "Eagle Lady" from Florida, received a young female golden eagle that had been the result of the artificial insemination of its mother. (Artificial insemination is often used in captive breeding programs for birds of prey; it is usually done with birds that are tame.) The bird lived with Doris for fifteen years and was the star of her bird-of-prey show until it died in 1996. Doris took this show to schools around the nation to teach people about the various birds of prey and their conservation. This golden eagle was probably seen by more Americans than any other eagle, even more than Old Abe, the famous Civil War bald eagle from Wisconsin.

gradually decreases until, by the time the eagle is an adult, it has disappeared altogether. The golden eagle does not get its full adult plumage until it is four years old or more.

Some golden eagles live year-round in or near their nesting territories. Others may migrate to different areas if they need to find more food during the winter. Unlike with bald eagles, migration distances usually are not great, and golden eagles do not move in large groups. Because of their excellent hunting abilities, they are able to survive in the mountains during the winter when bald eagles are forced to move to open water.

ABOVE: Golden eagles often assume this posture, called "mantling," when they have made a kill. The pose may help control struggling prey or hide prey from other eagles. Females often assume a similar posture over their young when disturbed on the nest. RIGHT: The golden eagle has been a symbol of honor and combat for centuries. This is the eagle represented in European heraldry, pictured on shields and as part of the crest of many noble families.

PAGES 98-99: Birds of open terrain, golden eagles are found in high mountains, and on plateaus, plains, and deserts. This one is in the Rocky Mountains of Colorado. Most often golden eagles hunt rodents and rabbits, but they may take insects, reptiles, and birds. They will eat carrion, especially when food is scarce in winter, but they prefer to hunt live prey.

ABOVE: This young golden eagle is showing that it feels threatened, probably because the photographer was too close for comfort.

OPPOSITE: White feathers in the plumage of a young golden eagle are progressively replaced by dark feathers at each molt. Final adult plumage may not be achieved for six to eight years, although birds usually begin to breed around age five.

ENDANGERED STATUS

CHAPTER

4

BEFORE EUROPEAN SETTLERS CAME TO NORTH AMERICA, THE BALD EAGLE WAS COMMON ACROSS MUCH OF THE CONTINENT. BUT OVER THE centuries, the bird became so rare that in the 1970s it was placed on the national list of endangered species. It wasn't until the middle of the twentieth century that the extent of the problem began to be known. In the 1950s, Charles Broley, who was banding nestling eagles in Florida, and Elton Fawks, who was watching the wintering eagles along the Mississippi River near Moline, Illinois, raised the alarm at the reduced numbers of eagles they were observing. In fact, there was great concern over the reduced numbers of many birds of prey, not just the bald eagle. The peregrine falcon was a species of extreme concern, and it actually became extinct on the East Coast.

Bald eagles have long been persecuted by man, especially where it was feared that the birds were competing with people for fish. Even today, with bald eagles protected by law, it is not uncommon to find birds injured by humans—sometimes accidentally, sometimes on purpose.

70

The National Audubon Society became aware of Mr. Broley's work in Florida and expressed its concern to the Fish and Wildlife Service. The Fish and Wildlife Service then turned to the National Audubon Society to manage the research, including the banding of the birds. Thus the National Audubon Society was responsible for coordinating many of the bald eagle recovery efforts during the 1960s.

Elton Fawks was one of the first men to publicly express his concern. In fact, Broley dubbed Fawks "the Paul Revere of the bald eagle decline." In 1961, to help document the bald eagle's decline, Fawks organized what has since become the annual Midwinter Bald Eagle Count, conducted by the Eagle Nature Foundation. This one- or two-day count is scheduled each year during the last weekend of January or the first weekend of February, after the southward migration has ended and before the northward migration has begun. To actually conduct the count, Fawks solicited the help of many individuals and of the Audubon and Conservation Clubs up and down the Mississippi River, as well as the Army Corps of Engineers personnel at each lock and dam. This count was the first real documentation that the bald eagle decline was widespread and

OPPOSITE: As land is cleared for agriculture and forests are cut for lumber, good nest sites have become rare, even as eagle populations recover and more nests are needed. In some areas, platforms mounted on poles have proved attractive to house-hunting eagles.

ABOVE: This bald eagle was found shot and brought to a rehabilitation center for veterinary care. If the injury is not crippling, the bird will be released after it heals. Volunteers all over the country give their time to rescue injured wildlife.

should be of national concern. Since there had been no previous counts of bald eagles, there were no good population numbers for comparison, but there was no doubt that the bird was vanishing. Fawks' count provided a reliable base line for future monitoring of the numbers of bald eagles.

The reasons for the decline of the bald eagle are complex, and there is no single cause. When Europeans first came to North America, bald eagles were fairly common. As the human population grew, the eagle population dwindled. People hunted and fished extensively, diminishing the food supplies for eagles and other birds of prey. Essentially, eagles and humans were in competition for the same food, and humans, with guns and traps at their disposal, had the upper hand. As the human population expanded westward, the eagles' natural habitats were destroyed, leaving them fewer places to nest and hunt. These two factors caused the population of bald eagles to decline sharply by the late 1800s.

By the 1930s, public awareness of bald eagles and their plight began to increase, and in 1940 the Bald Eagle Act was passed. This act somewhat reduced the pressures caused by humans, and eagle populations began to rebound. However, at the same time DDT and other pesticides began to be widely used, and these had a disastrous effect on birds of prey. Pesticides sprayed on plants were ingested by small vertebrates, which in turn were eaten by birds of prey. Thus birds of prey wound up with a concentration of poison in their systems, which harmed both the adult birds and the eggs that they laid. Pesticides caused bald eagles to lay eggs with very thin shells, so the eggs were often crushed when the birds tried to incubate them. Eggs that managed to stay whole during incubation often did not hatch, and government and private studies showed that these eggs contained extremely high levels of DDT and its derivatives. Bald eagle carcasses were also found to have large quantities of DDT stored in their fatty tissues and in their gonads, which possibly prevented the birds from laying fertile eggs or any eggs at all.

In the 1960s and early 1970s many states had placed the bald eagle on their lists of endangered species. Public awareness increased, and dedicated individuals and groups worked to make the conservation of eagles a national issue. On July 4, 1976, the Fish and Wildlife Service officially listed the bald eagle as a national endangered species.

Falconry is the sport and art of hunting with birds of prey. Falconers often work with chicks taken from the nest and have developed techniques for teaching such chicks to hunt. Modified, these techniques (called "hacking") have been used to release young golden eagles, bred and reared in captivity, into the wild. Young birds are housed and fed in a hacking tower like this one. As they learn to hunt, they gradually become independent.

The fact that the bald eagle was placed on the national endangered species list meant that all federal government agencies had to consider the bird and its habitat in all of their operations. It also meant that funds became available for more research on the bald eagle's changing population. Bald Eagle Recovery teams were appointed by the Fish and Wildlife Service to develop plans to help the bald eagle populations rebound in four regions of the country.

One of the first steps (and possibly the most important) taken by a government agency was the U.S. Forest Service's development of protective management guidelines for bald eagle nests on their forest lands. At the time this decision was made, close to eighty percent of all bald eagle nests were built on Forest Service land. The guidelines restricted human activity within half a mile (805km) of the nests during the nesting season. This helped to ensure the isolation of any young eagles that were hatched. It is believed that this protection of young eagles did more to bring back the dwindling bald eagle population than any other decree.

Another government agency that had a great effect on the bald eagle's recovery was the Environmental Protection Agency. With the formation of this agency and its directives, and the resulting cleaner water in American lakes and rivers, the bald eagle was once again able to hunt clean, healthy fish for itself and its young.

Once the bald eagle was placed on the national endangered list, many states started programs to restore the bald eagle within their own borders. A practice called hacking is used to return eagles to their natural habitats. Birds are raised in captivity but without any direct contact with humans, and they are trained to

This young golden eagle was hatched in captivity. It will be moved to a hacking tower around the time when it would normally leave the nest. Human caretakers provide food, but are careful not to be seen, so the young bird will not later approach people looking for a handout.

live in the wild. Once the birds are fully grown and able to hunt for themselves, they are released. New York was the first state to develop a hacking program for raising and releasing young bald eagles into the wild. The first eaglets were taken out of nests in Alaska, flown to the state of New York, and placed in hacking towers to prepare them for their eventual release.

This hacking program was so successful that other states emulated New York's efforts. Tennessee, Kentucky, Georgia, Missouri, Indiana, Massachusetts, and Oklahoma all developed hacking programs of some size. Some of the young eagles in the hacking programs were taken from nests in the wild in Alaska, Minnesota, Wisconsin, and Ontario, Canada. Others were produced by captive eagles in zoos such as the Cleveland Zoo in Ohio. Still others were raised by the Fish and Wildlife Service at its captive breeding facility in Patuxent, Maryland. Another group was pro-

OPPOSITE: Destruction of habitat continues to threaten the future of the bald eagle. Logging degrades watersheds, and lakes and streams become choked with silt. When water quality deteriorates, fish stocks disappear and so do bald eagles.

ABOVE: In his 1934 book *The American Eagle,* Francis Herrick said "In the course of fifty to sixty centuries the eagle has symbolized not only power, courage, and conquest, but freedom, independence, magnaminimity, truth, the soul of its bearer, the Holy Spirit, and immortality....Doubtless the greatest ignominy that the aquiline race has ever suffered at the hands of man was reserved for modern times."

duced by the George Miksch Sutton Avian Research Center in Oklahoma. Hundreds of young eagles have now been released through the state-subsidized programs.

A number of states used other methods to learn about and help preserve their eagle populations. Florida, Wisconsin, Michigan, and Minnesota all devoted manpower and aerial flights to monitor the bald eagle nesting areas for many years. And other states, including Illinois, Missouri, and Tennessee, monitored the bald eagles by flying over their wintering areas. Alaska and Texas have also played a role in the recovery of the bald and golden eagles by ending their bounties on these birds.

Arizona took a different approach to eagle preservation. The population in that state had dropped to approximately fifteen pairs, which produced only a dozen or so young each year. So the U.S. Forest Service in Tempe instituted a program of volunteers that would monitor each nest site. Getting people involved in protecting their local wildlife has proved to be an excellent conservation tactic, and in Arizona this intensive effort paid off as more and more eaglets were fledged each year. The Fish and Wildlife Service also committed several million dollars to a mammoth program of catching, banding, and radio-tagging every adult bald eagle nesting and every eaglet raised in Arizona. The results

Pesticides used on crops were not intended to injure eagles, but they did. Chemicals like DDT persist in an environment for many years, absorbed by plants and passed on in increasing doses to vegetarian animals and then to their hunters. DDT interferes with a female eagle's ability to protect her egg with a strong shell. When bald eagles exposed to pesticides tried to incubate, their eggs were crushed by the weight of the adult bird.

of that study showed that bald eagles from outside the study area were coming in and augmenting the resident population, which seemed to be gradually improving each year.

In fact, by 1996 most of these states had already reached the bald eagle population goals that they had hoped to achieve by the year 2000. The end result is that in 1995 the Fish and Wildlife Service reclassified the bald eagle to the status of "threatened" rather than "endangered" in most states. Some states, including Wisconsin, actually removed the bald eagle entirely from their list of threatened and endangered species. However, some bald eagle populations along the southern border of the United States are still considered endangered because Mexico continues to use harmful pesticides.

Because reintroduction efforts have been so successful, all of the hacking facilities are now closed, with the exception of one operated by the National Foundation to Save America's Eagles at Dollywood, near Pigeon Forge, Tennessee. This is the only facility where young eagles that are hatched in zoos or rehabilitated at the Raptor Rehabilitation Center in Minneapolis, Minnesota, can be accommodated. The success of the preservation efforts and the removal of the eagle from the endangered species list means that there are now very limited state and federal funds available to study and monitor the bald eagle and its habitat.

The dramatic recovery of the nation's bald eagle population has been the result of a combination of all the efforts on its behalf—from individuals, corporations, preservation groups, and state and federal government agencies. The bald eagle is a good example of what conservationists call an "umbrella" species: because it is dramatic and appealing to people, a tremendous effort has been made to preserve the bald eagle, and this has helped many other species that share the same habitat. If only we can keep nests protected from disturbances, food sources clean and reliable, and vital wintering habitats preserved and isolated from human activity, the bald eagle's future should continue to brighten.

Eagles can see a long distance, but they can't protect themselves against human ignorance, carelessness, and fear. The bald eagle is the symbol of a nation; its near disappearance was evidence of our mistreatment of nature, its resurgence a sign that it is not too late to try to fix the damage we have done.

THE FUTURE

C H A P T E R

5

THE FUTURE OF THE VARIOUS EAGLE SPECIES AROUND THE WORLD IS THREATENED. MOST OF THEM SEEM TO REQUIRE SOLITUDE AND DISTANCE from human development, so as humans expand into remote areas and destroy essential habitats and food sources, eagles are forced to continually move away from humanity. They must either adapt to the ever-changing environment or face extinction.

In North America, the golden eagle has been pushed back across the United States into the Rocky Mountains. Although this eagle appears to be holding its own, due to this area's remoteness, there are no accurate records of how strong the population is or how it is changing. Accurate counts are impossible; "educated" estimates are the best we can hope for.

We don't know how many bald eagles lived in North America at the beginning of the second millennium; one estimate suggests over 250,000. By the middle of the twentieth century, only a few thousand existed outside Alaska. The Bald Eagle Act of 1940, intended to protect the national bird of the United States, reduced intentional persecution at the same time that increasing use of pesticides loomed as the most deadly threat eagles had ever faced. With increased environmental awareness bald eagle numbers are also increasing.

We used to believe that we could get good estimates of bald eagle populations by counting them in their wintering areas. However, it has been documented that separate, experienced observers at the same location, within just a few minutes of each other, would record up to fifty percent more or fewer eagles than other observers. When this is extrapolated to include the whole wintering area, and then the whole continent, we find that it may not be possible to provide actual numbers.

Eagle species from other continents are not as well documented as the North American golden and bald eagles. But we do know that the habitats in which many of them live are being destroyed. Expansion of cities, clear-cutting of rain forests, and development of remote areas threaten the eagles' survival. Shooting, poisoning, pollution, drainage of wetlands, and pesticides also pose severe problems for eagle populations. Although the United States has banned usage of DDT on its own soil, it stills sells the pesticide to other countries.

However, there is hope. There are many efforts worldwide to protect segments of these endangered habitats so that eagles and other species will have places to live. The United States has set aside thousands of square miles for wildlife, preventing future exploration and development of these areas. This should protect the habitats and food sources that native golden eagles need for survival.

OPPOSITE: Difficult though it is to count or observe bald eagles, forest eagles are much harder to locate and follow. In countries around the world, people have begun to attempt this task, inspired by pride in the birds of their country, by love of nature, and by the knowledge that birds and humans face the same future.
ABOVE: Counting bald eagles is a daunting task. For much of the year, they live far apart, and their preference is to live far from man. Even when birds gather on wintering grounds, these areas may be hard to reach, and birds may move from day to day. It takes dedication and hard work to answer even simple questions about wildlife and wild habitats.

In Sweden, supplemental food is provided for the white-tailed sea eagle, which has reduced its winter mortality rate. Various countries in central Europe practice brood manipulation for the lesser spotted eagle. The chicks that hatch second are not likely to survive, so they are removed and placed in the nest of a more common species of bird. A week or two before fledging, when aggression among chicks diminishes, they are returned to their original nests.

The Harpy Eagle Conservation Programme works with South American governments, logging companies, and local people to protect harpy eagle nesting sites. The nests are monitored and chicks are radio-tracked to learn more about the ecology of the species, and a captive breeding program has been started.

The Madagascar Fish-Eagle Project tries to help local people find sustainable alternatives to habitat destruction and has created protected areas for the eagles. The Project also gets local people involved in studies of ecology and environmental management.

Conservationists in the Philippines have worked to change the name of their local eagle species from "monkey-eating eagle" to "Philippine eagle," which has helped to instill a sense of national pride in this unique native bird. The Philippine Eagle Program started a captive breeding program that is beginning to have some success, and it conducts nest monitoring and reforestation. This program even helped develop an "eagle" beer brand, to help keep the species in the public eye.

One way to study eagle flight is through radio telemetry. A radio transmitter, sometimes powered by solar batteries, is strapped around the wing near the shoulder. The transmitter emits a signal that can be picked up by trackers on the ground. The most recent (and expensive) transmitters broadcast to satellites, allowing birds to be tracked by computer.

Although eagle species (and in fact all birds of prey) are having tremendous difficulty around the world, concerned people have begun to make a difference. The success of the efforts to rebuild the North American bald eagle population is notable, and the fact that other countries and continents have begun to follow suit bodes well for the future. We must make sure that conservation efforts continue and grow even bigger, so that generations to come will be able to experience the beautiful sight of an eagle soaring on the wind.

ABOVE: We imagine flight to be effortless, but in reality it takes power and control. Humans are fascinated by flight, as the presence of many winged creatures in mythology and folklore attests.

OPPOSITE: This harpy eagle is a potent symbol for conservation, since it represents a complete ecosystem. This spectacular bird requires a healthy population of prey, which in turn requires a healthy forest. If we preserve the eagle, we also preserve its habitat and all other species that exist there.

PAGES 120-121: Eagles, especially hungry eagles, are early risers, using air currents produced by the morning sun to soar in search of prey. In the late afternoon, when the air becomes still, eagles doze while waiting for evening and the air currents generated by the cooling earth.

ABOVE: The future of any population lies in its young. This juvenile bald eagle must run the gauntlet of nature: it must learn to fly, hunt, find shelter, migrate, and mate. It also has to run the gauntlet of man, learning to avoid power lines, hunters, traps, and prey poisoned by lead shot. In nature, most eaglets don't survive to breed. When man modifies nature, fewer eaglets live to become eagles.

OPPOSITE: Is a population of eagles healthy? How do we know? For a population to remain stable, each pair of eagles must produce two young that survive to reproduce. This young bald eagle has passed its first tests: learning to fly and hunt. It will not be ready to attempt to breed until it is at least five years old.

PAGES 124-125: Conservation efforts require data. Are new pairs in an area moving in from other parts of the country, or are local birds producing enough young to make the population expand? Technologies for studying DNA are now so sophisticated that a bird's identity can be established from cells in a molted feather. Scientists can collect feathers from a nest or roost site, and answer important questions about bird populations without capturing or handling the birds they are studying.
ABOVE: Every year, thousands of amateur ornithologist participate in the Christmas Bird Count. Each team of birders is assigned an area, where year after year they record the abundance of each species they spot. This information provides evidence of population trends and can flag changes that might otherwise be overlooked.
OPPOSITE: Human population growth is the biggest current threat to the bald eagle, and to eagles around the world. Eagles need large, undisturbed spaces, whether they dwell in forests or on the steppe. They need clean water, healthy habitats, and undisturbed privacy. People need the same things. And unlike eagles, people can plan for the future and work for the good of their own species and that of others.

PAGES 128-129: The bald eagle is the one species of eagle found only in North America. Throughout its range, the bird has been persecuted by humans, hunted and poisoned, its habitat polluted and destroyed. Only humans can ensure that this magnificent bird survives.
ABOVE: This bird shows the dignity and pride that made the bald eagle the national symbol of the United States of America.
OPPOSITE: A few dark flecks among the white head feathers mark this bird as one just reaching adulthood. It is up to us to make sure that this bird and all other eagles have space to fly, hunt, and breed.

The wedge-tailed eagle is a close cousin of the golden eagle, and fills a similar role in its native Australia. The introduction of rabbits has been an ecological disaster for Australia, but one good thing has come of it: the wedge-tailed eagle population, which finds rabbits an ideal prey, has increased.

Man's attitude towards eagles is sometimes ambivalent—it can be hard to understand that predators play an important role in nature. Where predators disappear, ecosystems become less complex, and chain reactions cause plant species to disappear. The interrelationships in natural systems are hard to understand, until they are disrupted.

OPPOSITE: Silhouettes are simple, conservation is not. People share the world with wildlife. We must remember that natural resources are not free: there are costs associated with cutting forests, with mining minerals, and with consuming fisheries. If eagles disappear, can we be far behind?

ABOVE: In the United States, different communities have different names for the golden eagle. The bird is variously known as the American war bird, the bird of Jupiter, the royal eagle, and the King of Birds. We must make conservation efforts on this regal bird's behalf, just as we have successfully done for the bald eagle.

ABOVE: There are many people and organizations dedicated to helping eagles. If an injured eagle is rescued, there are people ready to help it heal. Sometimes injured birds recover but can't be released, because they can no longer survive without assistance. Many such birds, like this golden eagle, become ambassadors for their species, teaching both children and adults why eagles deserve a place on the earth.
OPPOSITE: Most people in the United States, given the choice, would choose eagles: they would want to keep habitats unspoiled and have a chance to see eagles fly free. We must make that choice and make it with action, to ensure that wildlife and wildlands survive for our own sake as well as for theirs.
PAGES 138-139: Eagles flew over the earth long before humans walked upon it. Monarchs of the sky, eagles remind us of our own potential for nobility, bravery, and truth. As we move toward the future, the flight of eagles is a promise that there is a place for us away from cities and cars, a place for us in nature. It is up to us to redeem that promise.

COMMUNITY of eagles is a group of eagles that winter, migrate, and nest in the same general area. This may be the result of family groups staying together.

DAYTIME ROOST is a tree in an isolated, somewhat sheltered location which is used by eagles during the day after they have fed, especially when there is disturbance at or near the feeding area.

EAGLE MIGRATION is a movement of eagles from one area to another, usually characterized by eagles moving in a straight line with wings half open, occasionally flapping or soaring to gain altitude.

EAGLE NEST STRUCTURE is a platform, tripod, or other man-made device upon which a dummy nest is placed to attract eagles to nest or to raise young eagles for release back into the wild.

EAGLE NEST TREE is a large tree with branches high above the ground that are sufficiently large and close together to support a nest which weighs hundreds of pounds.

EYRIE is a pile of sticks in a tree or on a rock cliff in which the eagles make a pocket or depression to lay their eggs. As the young get older, the depression disappears, and the nest becomes flat or even rounded on top.

FEEDING PERCH is a low limb, usually a short distance back from the edge of the trees, which is used by the eagles after capturing a fish or prey that is too large to eat while flying. It allows the eagles to eat without being disturbed.

HACKING is raising eagles in captivity in a man made structure, but without direct contact with humans.

NIGHTTIME OR MILD WEATHER ROOST is a group of trees, generally cottonwoods or oaks, which are isolated from human activity by at least a quarter mile (.4km) or by a physical barrier that hides them from sight.

OBSERVATION PERCH TREE is a tree close to a food source, either open water in which the eagles are fishing, or a carcass. This perch is used as the last stop before the eagles drop down to eat or fish.

OCCASIONAL FEEDING AREA is an area containing a temporary food source, which is used by the eagles for only a limited time. It may contain a temporary food source each winter or an opportunistic one-time food source.

PERCH TREE is a tree that is consistently used by one or more eagles for short periods of time.

POPULATION of eagles is composed of many community groups as well as individuals and encompasses a large geographic area. The habits and migrations of separate populations are definite and distinct from other populations.

REGULAR WINTER FEEDING AREA is an area that provides a consistent food source and is used by eagles all winter. Quite often this may be the open water below a dam or power plant.

ROOST is normally a group of trees, isolated from man's disturbances and protected from the weather, in which eagles spend the night.

SENTINEL PERCH is a tall tree close to or on the edge of a nighttime roost, which is used by an adult eagle (sentinel) that other eagles fly by on their way into the roost. If the sentinel has been disturbed and has flown from this perch, the other eagles will go on to another roost where the sentinel is still present.

SEVERE WEATHER ROOST is a group of trees which offers eagles protection from severe storms, particularly heavy winds. It is usually located along a valley wall or in front of a bluff. It is extremely important to the survival of eagles during severe winter weather as it minimizes energy loss.

SUNNING OR LOAFING PERCH TREE is a tree exposed to the sun, usually away from the feeding area, where the eagles can sit undisturbed for hours at a time, to sunbathe.